TABLE OF CONTENTS

#	SUBJECT	PAGE

TABLE OF CONTENTS

#	SUBJECT	PAGE

TABLE OF CONTENTS

#	SUBJECT	PAGE

TABLE OF CONTENTS

#	SUBJECT	PAGE

EXAMPLES OF LOG BOOKS YOU CAN CREATE

Create your own Log Book with this easy-to-use Multipurpose Log Book.
You can find below a couple of examples of how to create Column Headers for different needs.

Daily Activity Log Book

Create a Daily Activity Log Book to easily track your daily activities. Use the following prompts as column headers:

DATE	TIME	NAME	PHONE NUMBER	SUBJECT	FOLLOW-UP REQUIRED	INITIALS

Time Sheet Log Book

Create a Time Sheet Log Book to keep track of daily work hours, have everything in order, and get paid accordingly. Use the following prompts as column headers:

DAY	DATE	DESCRIPTION	TIME IN	TIME OUT	TOTAL HOURS	NOTES

Inventory and Equipment Log Book

Create an Inventory and Equipment Log Book to easily track inventory and equipment. Use the following prompts as column headers:

NO	DATE	ITEM DESCRIPTION	QUANTITY	PRICE	LOCATION	NOTES

Ledger Book or Income and Expenses Log Book

Create a Ledger Book to track your Income and Expenses easily so that you can stay in control of your finances.
Use the following prompts as column headers:

NO	DATE	DESCRIPTION	ACCOUNT	INCOME	EXPENSE	TOTAL

Mileage Log Book

Create a Mileage Log Book to easily track vehicle gas usage for tax reporting purposes. Use the following prompts as column headers:

DATE	TIME	DESTINATION	ODOMETER START	ODOMETER END	TOTAL MILEAGE	NOTES

Online Order Log Book

Create an Online Order Book to easily track online purchases. Use the following prompts as column headers:

NO	DATE	ITEM DESCRIPTION	ORDER #	COMPANY	AMOUNT	RECEIVED DATE

Donation Log Book

Create a Donation Log Book to easily track charitable donations. Use the following prompts as column headers:

NO	DATE GIVEN	ORGANIZATION/ INDIVIDUAL NAME AND DETAILS	DONATION (CASH, ITEMS)	VALUE	PAYMENT METHOD	TAX (Y/N) DEDUCTIBLE

Accounting Ledger Book

Create an Accounting Ledger Book to track easily finances and transactions. Use the following prompts as column headers:

NO	DATE	DESCRIPTION	ACCOUNT	DEBIT	CREDIT	BALANCE

Petty Cash Log Book

Create a Petty Cash Log Book to easily track your cash flow. Use the following prompts as column headers:

NO	DATE	DETAIL	CASH IN	CASH OUT	BALANCE	NOTES

Vehicle Maintenance Log Book

Create a Vehicle Maintenance Log Book to easily track maintenance and repair. Use the following prompts as column headers:

DAY	DATE	DESCRIPTION OF WORK DONE	MILEAGE	LOCATION/ COMPANY	REPLACEMENT PARTS	COST

Visitor Log Book

Create a Visitor Log Book to keep track of office guests and factory, company visitors. Use the following prompts as column headers:

NO	DATE	VISITOR'S NAME	REASON FOR VISIT	TIME IN	TIME OUT	SIGN/INITIAL

www.ingramcontent.com/pod-product-compliance
Lightning Source LLC
Chambersburg PA
CBHW051759200326
41597CB00025B/4612
9781803932217